THE
WHITE
WITCH

EMBODYING PURITY, HEALING, AND LIGHT

The White Witch: Embodying Purity, Healing, and Light

Copyright © Nichole Callaghan

Contents

Chapter 1: The Introduction to White Witchcraft

White witchcraft may conjure images of pure light, celestial beings, and all that is deemed as inherently good. It is a spiritual path that appeals to those who feel an innate calling to heal, to purify, and to shed light. But what exactly is white witchcraft? It is a blend of reverence for nature, belief in the intrinsic goodness of life, a commitment to personal and spiritual growth, and a mission to create a ripple effect of positive transformation in the world.

White witchcraft is a branch of the wider practice of witchcraft that emphasizes the use of magick for selfless purposes, healing, and the promotion of positivity and love. It draws on the belief in the interconnectedness of all things and the power of intention. By aligning themselves with the energy of purity, healing, and light, white witches, also known as lightworkers, serve as conduits of positive energy.

It is essential to clarify that the term "white" in white witchcraft is not indicative of race or ethnicity, nor does it suggest that other types of witchcraft are "dark" or "evil." Instead, the color white is symbolic. In many cultures, white represents purity, peace, healing, and illumination—principles that white witches uphold. Therefore, anyone, regardless of their race, gender, or cultural background, can practice white witchcraft if they resonate with these principles.

Moreover, white witchcraft does not conform to the stereotypical portrayal of witches, as propagated by pop culture and centuries of misunderstanding and prejudice. White witches do not deal with harmful spells, curses, or any form of manipulative magick that infringes upon free will. Their path is one of compassion, benevolence, and spiritual enlightenment.

Like other forms of witchcraft, white witchcraft is not a religion but a spiritual practice that can be incorporated into various faith systems. Some white witches may feel a close connection with Wicca, a modern pagan, witchcraft religion, while others may align their practice with their Christian, Buddhist, Hindu, or agnostic beliefs, among others. The beauty of white witchcraft lies in its adaptability and inclusivity.

In this spiritual journey, you will learn to tap into your intuition, connect with the energies around you, and channel them for healing, cleansing, and blessing. This path encourages personal development and spiritual growth, as it requires you to embody the principles of love, purity, and light in your everyday life.

The rituals and meditations included in this book will serve as tools to help you harness the energy of the universe, connect with your higher self, and transform your life and the lives of those around you positively. You will learn how to cleanse yourself of negative energy, channel healing, and shine your inner light. This path of spiritual development and magick is not just about performing rituals but about embracing a way of life that promotes harmony, balance, and positivity.

As you embark on this journey, it's crucial to approach it with an open mind and heart. Doubt and skepticism can serve as barriers to the flow of magickal energy. It is also vital to remember that practicing white witchcraft does not provide instant solutions to life's problems. Instead, it provides the tools and wisdom to face these challenges more effectively and to transform them into opportunities for growth.

White witchcraft is a practice that evolves with you, reflecting your personal growth and spiritual development. It is not about achieving a specific end goal, but about the journey itself—the daily efforts to live in alignment with the principles of purity, healing, and light, and the continuous learning and self-discovery that come along with it.

Embracing white witchcraft is embracing a call to be a source of love, healing, and light in the world. It is a commitment to promoting a greater understanding, peace, and unity. While the journey may not always be easy, the fulfillment derived from serving as a beacon of positivity is unparalleled.

Finally, remember that white witchcraft is a personal journey that is unique to each practitioner. There is no singular "right" way to practice, and what works for one person may not work for another. This book will provide guidelines and suggestions, but always listen to your intuition and adapt the practices to suit your unique spiritual needs and circumstances.

In the chapters to come, we will delve into the practices and principles of white witchcraft, starting with embodying purity. From there, we will explore healing, meditation, embracing the light, ethical considerations, the use of symbols and tools, creating sacred spaces, and more. By the end of this journey, you will have a foundational understanding of what it means to be a white witch, and more importantly, you will have begun a transformational journey of your own.

Embrace this path with curiosity, compassion, and a commitment to growth. Welcome to the world of white witchcraft. A world of purity, healing, and light awaits you.

Chapter 2:
Embodying Purity

Embodying purity is a fundamental element of white witchcraft. It represents not just physical cleanliness but more importantly, mental, emotional, and spiritual cleanliness. This chapter guides you on the path to understanding and embodying purity in the context of white witchcraft.

To embody purity as a white witch, you must live by the principles of love, kindness, honesty, and integrity. You must strive to make your intentions, thoughts, words, and actions as pure as possible. In essence, to embody purity is to live in harmony with your true nature, free from malice, deceit, or ill-intent.

The concept of purity in white witchcraft has been often misunderstood. Some believe it to be an absolute state of perfection, but this is a misconception. Embodying purity does not mean being flawless; it means striving towards betterment, nurturing your spiritual growth, and being authentic. It is a journey rather than a destination.

When you embody purity, you foster a deeper connection with the divine energy that permeates the universe. You become a conduit for positive energy, enabling you to effect healing and transformation, not just for yourself, but also for those around you.

Embracing Honesty

One of the first steps towards embodying purity is embracing honesty. Being honest means being true to yourself, others, and the universe. It is about aligning your thoughts, words, and actions. An honest person is someone whose words reflect their inner thoughts, and whose actions mirror their words.

However, embracing honesty is more than just telling the truth. It involves self-reflection and introspection. You need to be honest with yourself about your strengths, weaknesses, desires, and fears. Only by acknowledging and accepting these truths can you truly grow.

Living with Integrity

Living with integrity is another crucial aspect of embodying purity. Integrity involves being consistent in your principles, even when no one is watching. It is about upholding your ethical and moral standards regardless of the circumstances.

When you live with integrity, you generate a positive energy that radiates outward. This energy can purify the environment around you and have a profound impact on the people you interact with. Integrity acts as a beacon, guiding you on your path as a white witch.

Practicing Kindness

Another key aspect of embodying purity is practicing kindness. Kindness involves showing compassion and understanding to all living beings.

It also includes treating yourself with gentleness and care.

Practicing kindness opens your heart and increases your capacity to give and receive love. This, in turn, allows you to tap into the positive, healing energy of the universe more effectively. Moreover, being kind generates a ripple effect, impacting others and inspiring them to act kindly as well.

Nurturing Your Spiritual Self

To embody purity, you need to nurture your spiritual self. This involves taking time to meditate, reflect, and connect with the divine energy within you and in the universe. It also involves acknowledging and honoring the divine in others.

Nurturing your spiritual self requires discipline and commitment. It may involve setting aside time each day for meditation or spiritual practices, studying spiritual texts, participating in rituals, or engaging in acts of service.

As you nurture your spiritual self, you'll find yourself becoming more attuned to the energy around you. You'll become more intuitive, more empathetic, and more aware of the interconnectedness of all things. This awareness is a vital part of embodying purity.

Cleansing Rituals

Cleansing rituals are a practical way to embody purity. They allow you to clear negative energies from your body, mind, and spirit, and replace them with positive ones. These rituals can be as simple as taking a bath with salt and essential oils, smudging your living space with sage, or meditating with the intention of cleansing your aura.

Embodying purity as a white witch is a constant process. It requires continual self-reflection, honesty, integrity, kindness, and spiritual nurturing. As you cultivate these qualities and engage in cleansing rituals, you'll find yourself becoming a more effective conduit for divine, healing energy.

Remember that purity is not about being perfect; it's about striving to be the best version of yourself. It's about living authentically, with love, respect, and humility. As you continue on your journey as a white witch, may you find joy and fulfillment in embodying purity.

Chapter 3: The Path to Purity Ritual

White witchcraft embodies a deep respect and reverence for all forms of life and existence. At the heart of this practice lies the profound aspiration to embody purity - not in a sense of moral superiority or judgment, but as an embodiment of clear intentions, authentic actions, and harmonious existence. This path is neither quick nor easy, but it is transformative, leading to spiritual growth and enlightenment.

Embodying purity is about striving for inner cleanliness, clarity of thought, and ethical action. It's about aligning with the energies of the universe in a way that is positive and life-affirming. This chapter outlines a ritual designed to facilitate your initial step on this path. This ritual, known as the Path to Purity Ritual, is a purification ceremony that paves the way for spiritual cleansing and helps you align with the frequencies of white witchcraft. It's a way of sweeping away the old, making way for the new, and allowing the energy of purity to flow through your life.

The ritual involves three key stages: Preparation, Purification, and Affirmation.

Preparation

The first step in any ritual is preparation. Ensure you have a clean, quiet, and comfortable space for the ritual. This space should be one where you can feel relaxed and secure. Choose a time where you won't be disturbed, and gather your materials. For the Path to Purity Ritual, you will need:

A white candle to symbolize purity,

A bowl of pure water for cleansing,

A handful of sea salt or Himalayan salt, representing earth and purification,

Incense or sage for smudging,

Crystals like clear quartz or selenite that embody purity,

A piece of paper and a pen.

Once you have all your materials, take a few moments to ground yourself. Sit or stand barefoot on the ground, imagining roots extending from your feet into the earth, anchoring you firmly.

Purification

Begin the ritual by lighting the white candle. As you do, say the following words:

"By the light of this candle, I invite purity and clarity into my life."

Next, take the incense or sage and light it from the candle. As the smoke starts to curl upwards, gently waft it around your body, visualizing it purifying your aura and cleansing any negativity. As you do this, say:

"By the power of smoke and air, I cleanse myself of all that does not serve my highest good."

Take the bowl of water and add the salt, stirring until it dissolves. As you do this, visualize the water absorbing the purifying power of the salt. Dip your fingers in the water and lightly touch your forehead, heart, and solar plexus, saying:

"By the essence of salt and water, I cleanse my body, mind, and spirit."

Hold the clear quartz or selenite in your hands, feeling its pure and cleansing energy. As you hold it, imagine it radiating a white light that envelopes you completely, saying:

"By the energy of this crystal, I invite the light of purity into my life."

Affirmation

Finally, on the piece of paper, write down your intention to embody purity in your life. Be as specific as you can. You might write down something like, "I am living my life with purity, aligning my thoughts, words, and actions with my highest good and the good of all." Fold the paper three times and hold it in your hands. Close your eyes and spend a few moments focusing on this intention. Feel it in your heart, visualize it in your mind, and believe in its manifestation.

Open your eyes and place the folded paper under the candle. As the candle burns, it will further energize your intention. Keep the candle lit (safely) for as long as you can, ideally until it burns out.

To conclude the ritual, say:

"I have set on the Path to Purity. By the power of my will and the grace of the Universe, so it is."

Thank the universe, the elements, and the energies that have supported you in this ritual. Blow out the incense or sage, and keep the crystal and the piece of paper with your intention in a safe place, reminding you of your commitment to purity.

Remember, this ritual is not a magic solution, but a stepping stone on your path to purity. It's essential to back it up with everyday actions that support your intention. Strive to align your thoughts, words, and actions with purity. Be patient and kind to yourself on this journey. True transformation takes time.

Let this Path to Purity Ritual be a beacon, guiding you on your journey of white witchcraft, lighting your way with its pure and vibrant light.

As you walk this path, may you become a beacon of light, illuminating the way for others, embodying the true essence of a white witch - purity, healing, and light.

Chapter 4: Healing as a White Witch

In the spectrum of witchcraft, white witchcraft holds a distinctive place due to its focus on healing, light, and positivity. White witches, armed with compassion and purity, dedicate themselves to the craft of healing, providing solace to the world around them. This chapter delves into the role of healing within the realm of white witchcraft, discussing various forms of healing, from physical to emotional and spiritual.

The Essence of Healing

Healing, in its purest form, is about restoration—bringing something back to its natural state of health and harmony. It can involve repairing physical wounds, soothing emotional pain, or mending spiritual disconnections.

In the world of white witchcraft, healing is more than just a reactive response to injury or illness. It's an ongoing, proactive pursuit that aims to create an environment of wellness, peace, and equilibrium. It extends beyond the self, with many white witches seeking to promote healing in others, in nature, and in the world at large.

Physical Healing

The most commonly understood form of healing involves the body—addressing illness and injury to restore physical wellbeing. While white witches are not replacements for medical professionals, they often supplement conventional treatments with their practices, aiming to speed up recovery and boost overall health.

For example, a white witch may use herbs in their rituals, recognizing the healing properties these natural elements possess. Herbs like chamomile, lavender, and mint have been used for centuries to soothe various ailments, and in the hands of a white witch, they become part of a larger ritual of healing. The actual process could involve creating sachets, teas, infusions, or incense, with the specific choice depending on the person and their needs.

Emotional Healing

Beyond the physical realm, emotional wounds often run deeper and are less visible. Traumas, heartbreak, stress, anxiety—all these negative emotions can leave scars that need healing. White witches often serve as guides, leading those affected towards emotional recovery.

Here, the tools of a white witch may include crystals known for their emotional healing properties, such as rose quartz for heartache, or lapis lazuli for stress. Meditation, affirmations, and rituals of release may also be employed, aiming to let go of emotional pain and invite in positivity and peace. It's important to remember that, while these practices can be helpful, they're meant to complement professional mental health support, not replace it.

Spiritual Healing

At the core of white witchcraft is spiritual healing—repairing the disconnect between one's soul and the universe. This can manifest as feelings of emptiness, loss of purpose, or a general sense of being adrift. Spiritual healing seeks to restore that connection, helping individuals realign with their higher selves and the universe.

Spiritual healing often involves meditation, energy work, chakra balancing, and the use of tools such as crystals and herbs. Rituals can be designed to foster self-discovery, encourage spiritual growth, and facilitate a stronger connection to the divine or the universal energy that binds all living things.

The Healing Energy of a White Witch

Central to the healing work of a white witch is the concept of energy. Every living being, every object, and even every thought or emotion carries energy. Illness, emotional pain, or spiritual disconnect are often viewed as disruptions in this energy flow. A white witch works to realign and restore this flow, channeling positive, healing energy towards the areas of disruption.

Consider a garden with a stream running through it. If a rockslide obstructs the stream, plants may wilt, animals may leave, and the garden's health declines. Removing the obstruction and allowing the water to flow freely again restores life to the garden. Similarly, a white witch identifies and targets blockages in the energy stream, aiming to restore health, peace, and harmony.

The Ethos of Healing in White Witchcraft

As healers, white witches operate under an ethos of "do no harm." Their intention is always for the greater good, and they commit to respecting the free will and autonomy of those they assist. Healing, in the world of white witchcraft, is an act of love—an extension of the light that white witches seek to amplify in the world.

In the next chapter, we'll delve deeper into a specific healing ritual that you can practice to channel your energy towards healing, but for now, reflect on the broad concept of healing in white witchcraft. Understand its holistic nature—encompassing physical, emotional, and spiritual aspects. Realize the importance of energy in this process, and most importantly, remember the guiding principle of harmlessness that underpins all healing work of a white witch.

As you journey further into white witchcraft, let the ethos of healing guide you. Embrace your role as a healer—not just for yourself, but for those around you, and the world you inhabit. Through your actions, words, and intentions, strive to be a beacon of healing light in a world that so desperately needs it.

Chapter 5: The White Healing Ritual

Healing has always been a central part of witchcraft. In white witchcraft, particularly, the focus on healing is paramount. As a White Witch, you wield your energy, wisdom, and inherent magical abilities for the restoration of balance, health, and wellbeing, be it physical, emotional, or spiritual. This chapter provides a comprehensive guide to a healing ritual – a White Healing Ritual –

that will enable you to channel your energy towards healing yourself or others.

Before you begin, it's essential to remember that any healing ritual is not a substitute for conventional medical treatment. Instead, think of it as a complementary practice that can enhance the overall healing process by addressing aspects of wellbeing that mainstream medicine may overlook. Now, let us dive into the White Healing Ritual.

The White Healing Ritual

To perform this ritual, you will need a white candle, healing herbs (such as lavender, chamomile, or rosemary), healing crystals (like clear quartz or amethyst), and a piece of paper and pen.

Preparation

Begin by preparing your sacred space. Refer to Chapter 13 for more detailed guidance. Essentially, you want to create an environment that feels peaceful and safe, and free of distractions. Cleanse the area with sage, palo santo, or any method you prefer to rid it of negative energies. Then, set up your ritual tools: place your white candle in the center, surround it with your chosen healing herbs and crystals, and have your paper and pen ready.

Centering Yourself

To channel healing energy effectively, you must first be in a calm and centered state. Sit comfortably, close your eyes, and begin to focus on your breath. Take slow, deep breaths, filling your lungs fully and exhaling completely. As you breathe, envision a white light flowing into you with each inhale and any stress or negativity leaving you with each exhale. Do this until you feel calm and centered.

Setting Intentions

With your eyes still closed, ask yourself or the person you're healing: what needs healing? Listen to your intuition. Once you have identified what needs healing, open your eyes and write it down on the piece of paper. Fold the paper and place it near the white candle.

The Invocation

Light the white candle. As the flame flickers to life, visualize it as a beacon, radiating pure, healing energy. Say the following or similar words that resonate with you:

"In the name of the Great Spirit, by the power of the Earth, the air, the fire, and the water, I call upon the universal healing energy to flow through me and bring healing to [your name or the name of the person who needs healing]. May this light restore balance, bring comfort, and promote wholeness. So mote it be."

Channeling Healing Energy

This step requires focused intent and visualization. Close your eyes once more. Envision a brilliant white light emanating from the candle, growing larger with every breath you take. Picture this light encompassing you or the person you're healing, touching every cell, filling every space with its healing energy. As you do this, believe in the healing power you're channeling.

Completion

Once you feel that the healing energy has done its work, it's time to close the ritual. Thank the universal healing energy for its assistance. Let the candle burn down safely if you can, or extinguish it if you must. Dispose of the paper you wrote on by burying it in the earth, symbolizing the release of ailment and the acceptance of healing.

Healing doesn't happen overnight; it's a process. The White Healing Ritual can be performed as often as needed. Remember that your faith and positive intentions fuel the power of this ritual. It's not about perfection, but about love, compassion, and a genuine desire to bring about healing. Keep these things in mind, and you'll find your journey as a White Witch to be one of profound joy and deep satisfaction.

Finally, remember to treat yourself with the same loving kindness you offer others. Healing is, after all, a two-way street. As you heal others, you heal yourself; as you heal yourself, you make it possible to heal others. As a White Witch, you are not just a beacon of healing light; you're also a testament to the strength and beauty of a healed spirit.

You have begun your journey into the remarkable world of healing as a White Witch. As you continue, always remember that the light within you is the same light within others, and it is this interconnectedness that allows healing to occur. Embrace this truth, and let it guide you in your healing work.

In the upcoming chapters, we will explore the role of meditation in white witchcraft.

We will delve into guided meditations designed to foster purity and healing. Armed with the knowledge and power of these rituals and meditations, you can be the healing light you were always meant to be.

Chapter 6: Meditation and White Witchcraft

In the journey of the White Witch, meditation is an essential element. It's more than just a technique for relaxation or a method to deal with life's daily stresses; meditation is a fundamental tool in the witch's repertoire, a gateway to her true essence, and an anchor for her intentions. It allows her to access higher states of consciousness, tap into the divine, and channel purity, healing, and light.

Meditation, in essence, is a practice that involves focusing the mind to achieve a state of mental clarity and emotional calmness. It encourages a deep state of relaxation and tranquility, bringing about a sense of peace that radiates from the innermost essence of one's being. In the context of white witchcraft, meditation is the key to connecting with the universal energies of purity and healing, an essential component for embodying the light.

Meditation and White Witchcraft: The Intersection

White witchcraft is a path defined by its benevolent intentions, its dedication to healing, and its commitment to reflecting purity and light in all actions. Meditation complements this beautifully, allowing practitioners to sharpen their focus, fine-tune their intent, and nurture a deep, resolute inner peace. Through meditation, a White Witch can elevate her vibrations, attune herself to the frequencies of the universe, and manifest her desires in the material world.

Additionally, meditation fosters a deep sense of awareness. It allows witches to be fully present in the moment, acutely conscious of their thoughts, feelings, and the energy they radiate. This mindfulness is crucial in witchcraft, for a distracted or clouded mind can distort intentions and dilute the impact of rituals and spells.

The Role of Meditation in White Witchcraft

Meditation serves many roles in white witchcraft. Firstly, it is a tool for self-discovery. Through consistent practice, witches can peel back the layers of their consciousness, delve into their subconscious, and unearth their truest selves. Understanding oneself is vital to honing one's craft, for it allows for self-growth, empowers one's magic, and ensures one's actions are aligned with the higher self.

Meditation also cultivates inner peace and balance, creating a sanctuary within one's mind. This tranquility, this center of calm, is essential for conducting rituals and spells, for it ensures that the witch's intentions are pure, her focus sharp, and her energies unclouded by negative emotions.

Furthermore, meditation can serve as a means to communicate with the divine. By quieting the mind and tuning into the subtle energies that surround us, witches can receive messages, guidance, and wisdom from higher planes of existence. This divine communion can provide invaluable insights and a broader perspective, influencing the witch's practices and shaping her spiritual journey.

Incorporating Meditation into Your Practice

Incorporating meditation into your white witchcraft practice need not be complicated. Here are a few guidelines to help you get started:

Establish a Routine: Consistency is key in meditation. Establish a routine that suits your lifestyle. You may choose to meditate once a day, twice a day, or perhaps only a few times a week. The frequency is less important than the regularity of your practice.

Choose a Quiet Place: Select a space where you feel comfortable and at peace. This could be a dedicated corner in your home, a quiet spot in your garden, or even a peaceful outdoor location. The important thing is that it should be a place where you can meditate without being disturbed.

Focus on Your Breath: A common technique to start with is focusing on your breath. Breathe in deeply, hold for a moment, then exhale slowly. Repeat this cycle, allowing your mind to quieten and your thoughts to settle.

Set an Intention: Before you begin each session, set an intention. This could be anything from seeking guidance, healing a specific emotional wound, manifesting a desire, or simply finding inner peace.

Be Patient: It's important to be patient with yourself. Meditation is a practice, and it may take time to see progress. Don't be discouraged if your mind wanders or if you find it difficult to focus initially. Remember, the journey is just as important as the destination.

In the realm of white witchcraft, meditation is not only a path to tranquility but also a means to empowerment. It fosters self-awareness, enhances focus, facilitates divine communication, and underpins the practice of magic with clarity and purity. By incorporating meditation into your witchcraft practices, you open up a world of profound self-discovery, cosmic connection, and magical potential. Let the stillness of your mind be your guide as you tread the path of the White Witch, embodying purity, healing, and light.

Chapter 7: Guided Meditations for Purity

In the spiritual lexicon of the White Witch, purity does not mean being untouched or undefiled. It means living in alignment with your highest self, unclouded by negative energies and influences. This purity is what we're aiming to reach through our meditations. Meditation is the process of turning inwards, of aligning your mind, heart, and spirit in harmony with the universal energy, and the practice of meditation allows us to embrace our essence in its most unadulterated form.

Meditation in white witchcraft is a means of self-exploration and self-improvement. It's a tool that allows us to clear our energy fields and live in a state of purity, ever-connected to our truest selves. This chapter will guide you through three specific meditations intended to enhance your purity, focusing on the self, the home, and the universe. Each meditation has been designed with the core principles of white witchcraft in mind and will allow you to further align with the path of light and healing.

Self-Purification Meditation

The first meditation is the Self-Purification Meditation, a tool to cleanse your energy, to wash away negative emotions, thoughts, and energies that might have attached themselves to you.

Begin by finding a calm, quiet space where you will be undisturbed. Settle into a comfortable position, either sitting or lying down. Close your eyes and take a few deep, cleansing breaths. Inhale peace and exhale any tension or stress.

Visualize a bright white light above your head. This light is pure and cleansing. As you continue to breathe, imagine this light beginning to descend, enveloping you in its radiant glow. Let it wash over you, entering from the top of your head and flowing all the way down to your toes.

As this light passes through each part of your body, visualize it sweeping away any negativity, any ill-will, any grudges, or harmful thoughts you may have been holding onto. Feel these negative elements disintegrate under the power of the pure white light.

Repeat this process until you feel fully cleansed and bathed in the white light. You may feel lighter, more at peace, more in tune with your higher self. Once you feel complete, gently bring yourself back to your surroundings and open your eyes.

Home-Purification Meditation

Our homes are extensions of ourselves. If we wish to embody purity, our living spaces must also reflect that. The Home-Purification Meditation aims to cleanse your surroundings and infuse them with pure, positive energy.

Begin by finding a quiet spot in your home. Close your eyes, take a few deep breaths, and center yourself. Visualize your home as it is, with its familiar rooms and furnishings.

Now imagine a bright, purifying white light starting at the base of your home. Visualize it moving upward, like a flood of positive energy, filling each room as it ascends. This light illuminates every corner, dispelling shadows and cleansing each space of any negative energy.

Picture this light permeating every object, every wall, every piece of furniture. It purifies and blesses everything it touches, leaving each room filled with tranquillity and purity. Feel this shift in energy and relish in the sensation of living in a cleansed, harmonious space.

Once the light has flooded your entire home, sit with this new energy for a moment. Open your eyes when you're ready, and try to retain this sensation of purity as you go about your daily life.

Universal-Purification Meditation

The final meditation focuses on connecting with the universe and its boundless energy. The aim is to feel our place in the cosmos, and in doing so, understand the inherent purity of our existence.

Begin as always by finding a quiet place where you won't be disturbed. Close your eyes, and visualize the Earth as seen from space, radiant and beautiful.

Now imagine a radiant white light emanating from the planet, stretching out into the universe, reaching stars, planets, galaxies. Visualize this light as a symbol of purity, a beacon of love and positivity extending from our shared home.

Feel your connection to this light, your role in the grand scheme of the universe. Realize that you, like the Earth, are full of energy, light, and love. You are a being of purity, contributing your unique energy to the cosmos.

Hold onto this visualization, this sense of unity and purity, as long as you need. When you're ready, bring yourself back to your surroundings, carrying this sense of connection and purity with you.

Through these meditations, we channel the essence of white witchcraft, bringing ourselves closer to the ideals of purity, love, and light. Like any skill, meditation requires practice. The more you meditate, the more adept you become at reaching that state of purity swiftly and effortlessly.

Remember, the purpose of these meditations is not to strive for an impossible standard of perfection but to bring you closer to your true self, your pure self. So, let's tread this path together, hand in hand with purity, walking towards healing and light.

Chapter 8: Guided Meditations for Healing

In the practice of white witchcraft, meditation holds a special place as it is considered a direct route to tap into the universal energies of purity, healing, and light. Meditation is not only a practice of the mind, but also of the spirit. It is a tool for healing, not only for ourselves but for others too. We've already discussed guided meditations for purity in the previous chapter.

Now, let's focus on guided meditations designed to promote healing.

The process of healing is a deeply personal and individual journey. While there are numerous external factors that contribute to our overall well-being, the power of the mind is a critical element that is often overlooked. Healing meditations are a tool to tap into this power, focusing our internal energy towards the healing process.

Introduction to Healing Meditation

Healing meditations help in two major ways: self-healing, where we focus on healing our own physical, emotional, and spiritual wounds, and distant healing, where we direct our energies to help heal others.

Before we delve into specific healing meditations, it's important to understand the structure and technique behind them. A healing meditation usually begins with entering a meditative state, which means finding a calm and quiet space, both externally and internally. This state can be achieved through deep and conscious breathing, visualization, and sometimes with the aid of meditative music or sounds.

Once we're in the meditative state, the healing process can begin. This is usually done through focused intention and visualization. We visualize the healing energy as a brilliant, pure light, often white or golden, emanating from within us or coming down from the universe, and directed towards the areas of the body, mind, or spirit that require healing.

Healing Meditation 1: Self-Healing through the Chakras

The first meditation we're going to explore is designed for self-healing through our chakras, the seven main energy centers within our bodies according to ancient Eastern philosophy.

Begin by sitting or lying comfortably in a quiet space where you won't be disturbed. Close your eyes and take a few moments to settle into your body. Breathe deeply and slowly, letting your awareness fully inhabit the present moment.

Starting from the base of your spine, visualize the first chakra, the Root Chakra. See it as a vibrant, spinning red disk of energy. As you inhale, visualize a brilliant white light pouring into this chakra, purifying and healing it. As you exhale, visualize any physical, emotional, or spiritual blockages dissolving and leaving your body.

Repeat this process with each chakra, moving up through the Sacral Chakra (orange), Solar Plexus Chakra (yellow), Heart Chakra (green), Throat Chakra (blue), Third Eye Chakra (indigo), and finally the Crown Chakra (violet). Take your time with each chakra, allowing the healing light to thoroughly cleanse and heal.

After you've completed this process with all seven chakras, spend a few moments visualizing your entire body, mind, and spirit as radiant with the healing light. Allow this light to expand beyond your physical body, enveloping you in a healing aura.

Gently bring your awareness back to your physical surroundings, carrying with you the healing energies cultivated through this meditation.

Healing Meditation 2: Distant Healing Meditation

This next meditation is focused on sending healing energies to another person. It is a practice of empathy, love, and light that extends the principles of white witchcraft beyond ourselves.

Begin just as you did in the self-healing meditation, by finding a comfortable position in a quiet place, closing your eyes, and focusing on your breath.

Visualize the person you want to send healing energy to. Picture them in your mind as vividly as you can. See them smiling, laughing, fully healthy, and vibrant.

Picture a ball of brilliant, healing light in your heart. With every inhale, see this light growing brighter and stronger. With every exhale, imagine sending this light towards the person you are healing.

Visualize this healing light entering their body, illuminating them from within, reaching every cell, every organ, every part of their body that needs healing. See them basking in this light, see their body accepting this healing energy.

Once you have visualized the light completely filling their body, see it envelop them, creating a protective and healing aura around them.

Slowly bring your focus back to your own body and the room you are in. Remember that while you can send healing energy, the acceptance and use of this energy depends on the receiver.

These meditations should be practiced with patience and regularity. Healing, whether of ourselves or others, is a gradual process. The more consistently you practice, the more you'll develop your ability to channel healing energies.

In the next chapters, we'll delve deeper into the practical aspects of white witchcraft, exploring tools, rituals, and spaces that aid in our journey towards embodying purity, promoting healing, and embracing the light. Remember, as white witches, our path is one of love, peace, and healing. Through our practices, we aim to bring more of these qualities into our world.

Chapter 9:
Embracing the Light

Throughout our journey into the realms of White Witchcraft, we have delved into the importance of embodying purity, engaged in healing practices, and explored the quiet power of meditation. This chapter draws us towards a critical and defining feature of the White Witch: the ability to embrace the light.

Embracing the light is more than just a metaphor; it represents a critical mindset, a spiritual stance, and a way of life for the White Witch. It is about understanding that light exists within every life form and everything in the universe and learning how to tap into this energy. It's about letting this light guide you, becoming a beacon of positivity, healing, and hope for yourself and others.

Embracing the light - a simple phrase, yet it carries a profound meaning that holds the potential to revolutionize your life and spiritual journey. It takes courage, commitment, and continuous effort. In this chapter, we will help you uncover this concept in its entirety.

Understanding the Light

Light, in the context of White Witchcraft, transcends its physical definition. It refers to the pure, vibrant energy that underlies all existence. This energy is filled with love, hope, positivity, and potential. As we embrace the light, we align ourselves with these qualities and aim to reflect them in our lives.

Embracing the light is also about understanding and accepting the dual nature of existence. Just as the physical world has day and night, light and dark, the spiritual world echoes this duality. Light and shadow are not adversaries but complementary aspects of life. Recognizing this balance is vital, but as White Witches, we consciously choose to align with the light while acknowledging the darkness.

The Role of Light in White Witchcraft

The light is the very heart of White Witchcraft. It underpins the concepts of purity and healing, both central to the path of the White Witch. The light purifies, cleanses, and brings clarity, helping us discard what no longer serves us. It is a source of profound healing, bringing solace to the weary and hope to the desolate.

Light also symbolizes knowledge and enlightenment. The term "illumination" is used to describe the state of gaining spiritual insight, highlighting light's role in our journey towards wisdom and understanding. As White Witches, we strive for this illumination, seeking to gain a deeper understanding of ourselves, others, and the universe.

Embracing the Light: A Personal Journey

Every person's journey to embrace the light is unique, reflecting their life experiences, perceptions, and spiritual aspirations. It is a personal journey, yet it carries a universal resonance. Embracing the light transforms our consciousness, our actions, and our interactions.

The journey begins with self-awareness. The more we understand ourselves - our thoughts, emotions, and patterns - the more equipped we are to usher in the light. Engage in introspective practices, like journaling and meditation, and consider your actions and reactions.

As we embrace the light, we also strive to embody it, reflecting it in our actions. This embodiment means leading a life of kindness, compassion, and respect for all living beings. It means walking the path of truth, standing up for justice, and helping those in need. It also means nurturing our wellbeing and practicing self-love, for the light within us must be strong and steady to illuminate the world around us.

Practices for Embracing the Light

Here are some spiritual practices that can help you embrace the light:

Light Visualization: Visualization is a powerful tool in White Witchcraft. Picture a radiant light within you, in your heart or your solar plexus. Imagine it growing brighter with each breath, filling your entire being and extending outwards. Practice this daily, especially during meditation.

Affirmations: Positive affirmations can help align our thoughts with the light. Phrases like "I am a beacon of light and love," or "I embrace the light within me," when repeated regularly, can affect our subconscious, aligning our thoughts and actions with the light.

Working with Light Energies: This involves working with energies that symbolize light. These can include elements like fire or crystals like clear quartz and selenite that are known for their light-bearing properties.

Engaging in Light-filled Activities: Participating in activities that bring joy, peace, and positivity can help you embrace the light. These activities could be anything from painting, gardening, dancing, to helping a neighbor, volunteering, or practicing yoga.

Mindful Living: Being present and mindful in each moment allows us to recognize and choose the light in our daily decisions. Mindfulness brings clarity, helping us distinguish between actions that contribute to our light and those that diminish it.

Embracing the light, Radiating the light

As we succeed in embracing the light, an amazing transformation begins. We not only hold the light within us but start to radiate it. We become beacons, illuminating our path and helping others find their way. We become agents of healing, channels of love, and catalysts for positive change.

Embracing the light is an enriching journey, a continuous process of personal and spiritual growth. Remember, the path to the light is not always easy; it requires patience, perseverance, and a generous dose of self-love. But the rewards are beyond measure. As you progress, you will discover a sense of peace, fulfillment, and joy that transcends the mundane and brings a profound sense of purpose and connectedness to your life.

May your path be illuminated, your journey be filled with love, and may you find the courage to embrace and embody the light.

Chapter 10: Ritual of the White Light

The Ritual of the White Light is a crucial practice for those who follow the path of the white witch. It is a powerful technique designed to enable you to connect with the divine light within you and the energy that surrounds you. This ritual can be used for various purposes, from healing to purification, from manifesting positivity to cultivating spiritual growth.

Before we delve into the details of the ritual, it's essential to understand what we mean by "White

Light". In the context of white witchcraft, White Light refers to the pure, divine energy that permeates the universe. It is seen as the source of all life, love, peace, and wisdom. This Light isn't associated with any particular religious belief or deity. Instead, it represents the highest form of spiritual energy, pure, and untainted.

The Ritual of the White Light is a practice that opens up the conduit between you and this divine energy. It allows the Light to flow into you, purifying your aura, healing your spirit, and radiating outward to impact the world around you. It is a celebration of the divine, an intimate connection between you and the universe.

Now, let's discuss the steps involved in the Ritual of the White Light.

Preparation

Every powerful ritual starts with preparation. First, you need to choose a quiet and comfortable space where you won't be disturbed. This could be a dedicated room, a corner of your home, or even an outdoor space that feels sacred to you. If you have a permanent altar set up, that's wonderful, but it's not necessary. What's more important is that the space feels peaceful and conducive to spiritual work.

Before starting the ritual, cleanse this area. You might use a smudge stick, a bell, or a broom—pick a cleansing method that resonates with you. This cleansing process helps eliminate any negative or stagnant energies, preparing the space for positive, divine energy to flow in.

Dress in comfortable, clean clothes. White is an appropriate color for this ritual as it symbolizes purity and light. Sit or stand in your space, whichever feels more comfortable to you.

Opening the Ritual

Begin by grounding yourself. You can do this by visualizing roots growing from your feet and burrowing deep into the earth. Feel your connection to the earth, and feel the energy from the earth flowing up into your body.

Once you feel grounded, cast a circle around your space. You can do this by envisioning a sphere of white light surrounding you. This circle serves as a barrier to protect you from negative energies during your ritual.

Now, take a moment to set your intention for the ritual. Are you seeking healing? Do you wish to cleanse your aura? Are you hoping to radiate positivity around you? Whatever it is, state your intention clearly and firmly, either out loud or in your mind.

The Ritual

With your intention set, close your eyes and take a few deep breaths. Let go of any thoughts or worries from your day and focus on the present moment.

Start visualizing a brilliant white light above you. This light is pure, warm, and inviting. Feel its warmth and love as it begins to descend towards you. As it reaches you, let it envelop you completely, from the crown of your head to the soles of your feet. Feel the energy of the White Light infusing into every cell of your body.

Feel the White Light purifying your mind, your body, and your spirit. Let it wash away any negativity or impurities that you've been carrying. If you're seeking healing, visualize the Light mending your wounds and soothing your pains.

Now, imagine the Light radiating outward from you, filling the room, and then expanding beyond the walls of your home. Let it fill your neighborhood, your city, your country, and finally, the entire planet. Envision the White Light wrapping the Earth, healing and purifying all life on it.

Stay in this state for as long as you wish, radiating the White Light and feeling its divine energy flowing through you.

Closing the Ritual

When you're ready, start withdrawing the Light back into you. Visualize it receding from the planet, back into your city, your neighborhood, your home, and finally, back into your being.

Express your gratitude for the White Light and the divine energy it has brought into your life. Thank the universe for connecting with you and working through you.

Slowly dissolve the circle of protection around you, and ground yourself once more, feeling your connection to the earth.

Open your eyes when you're ready. Take a moment to sit in silence, reflecting on your experience and the feelings that the ritual brought up for you.

Reflection

The Ritual of the White Light is a powerful practice for white witches. It allows us to connect with the highest form of spiritual energy, healing ourselves, and the world around us. But remember, magic doesn't end when the ritual ends. As you go about your day, carry the White Light within you. Let it guide your actions, infuse your interactions with love and positivity, and shine through you into the world.

Remember that this ritual is not a one-time event. It's a practice that you can return to time and time again, whenever you feel the need to reconnect with your divine energy. As with any practice, the more you engage with it, the deeper and more powerful your experiences will become. The Ritual of the White Light is a gift, a tool that empowers you to tap into your inner divinity and let it shine out into the world. Use it wisely, and with love.

Chapter 11: Ethical Considerations for White Witches

While white witchcraft revolves around the principles of healing, purity, and light, it's essential that those on this path also understand the importance of ethics in their practice. This chapter will delve into the ethical implications of white witchcraft, emphasizing the significance of intent, respect for free will, and the fundamental "do no harm" principle.

Ethics in any sphere of life provides a moral compass to guide our actions, and witchcraft is no exception. In the context of white witchcraft, ethical considerations help ensure that our actions align with the tenets of love, light, and healing. These considerations protect not only the practitioners but also those around them from potential harm.

Firstly, let's discuss the concept of intent. Intent refers to the purpose or reason behind our actions. It's the driving force behind our rituals, spells, and meditations. The energy of intent has immense power and influences the outcome of our witchcraft practices. For white witches, the intent should always be positive, aiming to bring about healing, peace, and harmony. Any intent that seeks to cause harm, manipulate, or control others contradicts the principles of white witchcraft.

Consider this scenario: A friend is going through a tough breakup and is in immense emotional pain. As a white witch, you want to help. A positive, ethical intent would be to cast a spell or conduct a ritual that aids their healing process, encourages emotional resilience, and imbues them with strength and hope. An unethical intent would be to cast a spell to manipulate their ex-partner's emotions or decisions. It's important to remember that your role is to foster healing and positivity, not to interfere with another's free will.

This brings us to the second point, respecting free will. Everyone has the right to make their own decisions, to feel their emotions, and to live their lives as they see fit. As a white witch, it's crucial to respect this. We may not always agree with someone's choices, but we must honor their autonomy. Attempting to control, manipulate, or force another person into a particular course of action infringes upon their free will, which is unethical.

The last critical ethical principle in white witchcraft is the axiom "do no harm." This is a common tenet across many spiritual and magical traditions, encapsulated in the Wiccan Rede's phrase, "An it harm none, do what ye will." The idea is simple yet profound: whatever you do, ensure it doesn't harm others or yourself. This harm can be physical, emotional, or spiritual.

White witches must also extend this principle to their healing practices. If you're performing a healing ritual or spell for someone, always seek their consent. Just as medical practitioners require informed consent before any treatment, so too should you before performing any healing practices. In addition, ensure that your magical healing practices don't replace or interfere with any medical treatment they're receiving. White witchcraft can complement medical treatment but should never replace professional medical advice.

Aside from these primary principles, other ethical considerations come into play. Respect for nature and all living beings is paramount. This respect influences the tools you choose and how you source them. For instance, a white witch should strive to use ethically sourced herbs and crystals, avoiding any that exploit human labor or harm the environment.

Additionally, respecting other's beliefs and practices is crucial. While you have chosen the path of a white witch, understand that others may have different spiritual or magical practices. Avoid passing judgment or attempting to enforce your views on them.

Ethics in white witchcraft extends beyond your personal practice. How you teach others (should you choose to) and how you represent witchcraft to those who do not practice are also matters of ethical importance. Be honest about your practices, dispel myths and misconceptions where you can, and always present witchcraft in a light that is true to its healing and loving nature.

Being a white witch is not just about performing rituals, meditations, and spells. It's about embodying the values of love, light, healing, and purity in all aspects of life. It's about living ethically, making choices that respect the free will of others, and striving to bring about positive change without causing harm. By adhering to these ethical considerations, you ensure that your journey as a white witch is as fulfilling and beneficial as possible for both yourself and the world around you.

Chapter 12: Tools and Symbols of White Witchcraft

In the practice of white witchcraft, tools and symbols are integral. They serve as physical representations of our spiritual intentions, helping to focus our energy and manifest our desires. This chapter will delve into various tools and symbols commonly utilized in white witchcraft and explain how they enhance our rituals and meditations.

Wands

Wands are traditional tools in many magical traditions. They are often used to direct energy, representing the element of air or fire, depending on the tradition. For a white witch, a wand can be a powerful tool for manifesting healing and purity. Wands can be made from a variety of materials, but those fashioned from natural elements such as wood are particularly potent. A wand made from willow, for instance, is believed to enhance healing and protection.

Candles

Candles are indispensable tools for white witchcraft. They are used in various rituals and meditations, symbolizing the light that we aspire to embody. Different color candles represent different energies: white candles are often used for purification and healing rituals, pink for love and compassion, and green for growth and renewal.

Crystals

Crystals are revered in white witchcraft for their healing properties. Each crystal possesses unique energies and can be used for different purposes. Clear quartz, for instance, is a versatile crystal known for its purifying and amplifying properties. Rose quartz is associated with love and emotional healing, while amethyst is thought to promote spiritual growth and protection.

Pentacle

The pentacle, a five-pointed star within a circle, is a prevalent symbol in witchcraft. It represents the four elements—earth, air, fire, water—crowned by spirit. For white witches, the pentacle often symbolizes the balance and harmony of these forces within the universe and ourselves.

Athame

The athame is a ceremonial knife used in various witchcraft traditions. Unlike a wand, it is never used to direct energy but instead for cutting energetic ties or opening and closing circles. In white witchcraft, an athame is often used symbolically, reflecting our ability to sever negative influences and maintain spiritual boundaries.

Chalice

The chalice, or cup, symbolizes the element of water and is often used in rituals involving emotional healing and intuition. It can hold water, wine, or herbal infusions during rituals and represents the divine feminine, the womb of the mother, and the flow of emotions and intuition.

Herbs and Incense

Herbs and incense are used in white witchcraft for their energetic properties. For instance, lavender is renowned for its calming and healing properties, while sage is often used for purification and protection. Burning specific herbs or incense during rituals and meditations can help create a conducive atmosphere for your intentions.

Book of Shadows

A Book of Shadows is a personal journal where witches record their rituals, spells, and thoughts. In white witchcraft, this book serves as a sacred repository for your journey, including your experiences with embodying purity, promoting healing, and embracing light.

Cauldron

Representing the divine feminine and the element of water, the cauldron is a symbol of transformation and rebirth. It is used for brewing potions, burning herbs or papers, and in symbolic rituals representing the transformative power of the divine feminine.

While these are common tools in white witchcraft, remember that the most important element is not the tools themselves, but your intent. Tools and symbols serve to help focus your intent and connect you physically to the spiritual realm, but they are not the source of your power. You are.

As a white witch, your journey is about channeling the inherent purity and light within you. In all your practices, keep this in mind. The rituals, the meditations, the symbols, and tools—they are all pathways to help you connect with your higher self and the universal energies of love and healing.

In choosing your tools and symbols, be guided by your intuition. No one tool or symbol is universally right for everyone. Instead, choose what resonates with you, what helps you focus your energy and intentions. Remember, the most effective tools and symbols are those that help you align with the essence of white witchcraft— purity, healing, and light.

Lastly, treat your tools with respect. They are extensions of your spiritual practice. Cleanse them regularly to keep their energy pure, and store them respectfully when they are not in use. The more you work with them, the more attuned they will become to your unique energy, thereby becoming more effective aids in your magical workings.

Now that you are familiar with the different tools and symbols of white witchcraft, the next chapter will guide you through creating a sacred space—a place where you can perform your rituals and meditations with focused intent, free from distractions, and aligned with the energies of purity, healing, and light.

Chapter 13: Creating a Sacred Space

As you journey further into your practice of white witchcraft, you will realize the importance of cultivating a sacred space. This is more than just a physical location; it is an extension of your spirit and a testament to your commitment to the path of purity, healing, and light. It is a sanctuary for your soul, an oasis of tranquility and peace where your spiritual energies can flow freely, unimpeded by the outside world.

Creating a sacred space requires thoughtful consideration, intentional planning, and a deep respect for the spiritual energies at play. It demands sincerity in your efforts to harmonize with the universe, the earth, and all the forces that guide your craft. This chapter will guide you through the process of creating your sacred space.

What is a Sacred Space?

In the context of white witchcraft, a sacred space is a dedicated area where you perform rituals, meditations, and other spiritual activities. The aim of this space is to provide an environment that resonates with purity, healing, and light - the core principles of your practice.

This space doesn't necessarily have to be vast or grandiose. It could be a small corner in your room, a section of your garden, or even a designated spot in your local forest. The key is that this space should make you feel connected, grounded, and at peace. It should inspire introspection, facilitate spiritual growth, and serve as a conduit for your magical energies.

Choosing Your Sacred Space

The choice of your sacred space should be guided by intuition. Listen to your inner self; it often knows where you feel most connected and calm. It should be somewhere you can have privacy, as the nature of your craft requires solitude and silence.

When choosing your space, consider the sensory experience - how does it smell, sound, feel? Are there any distracting noises or smells? The space should stimulate your senses in a way that promotes tranquility and focus. Perhaps the sound of a running brook calms your mind, or the scent of pine needles helps you connect with the earth. Trust your senses and let them guide you.

Cleansing Your Space

Once you've chosen your space, it's crucial to cleanse it. Remember, the purpose of cleansing is to remove any negative or stagnant energies that might hinder your practice. For this task, you could use a variety of techniques. Some witches prefer to use sage or other herbs for smudging, while others use sound vibrations from bells or singing bowls. Choose a method that resonates with you.

Visualize the smoke or the sound waves sweeping away any negative energies as you move around your space. Affirm your intention for this space to serve as a beacon of light, purity, and healing.

Setting Up Your Space

After cleansing, you can begin setting up your space. Start by adding an altar. This will serve as the focal point of your rituals and practices. Your altar can be a small table, a shelf, or even a cloth laid on the ground.

Next, add the tools you will be using in your practice. These might include a white candle (representing light and purity), crystals like selenite or clear quartz (for their healing and cleansing properties), and any other symbols of white witchcraft that you feel connected to.

Remember to arrange your tools in a way that is aesthetically pleasing and symbolically meaningful to you. You may want to incorporate the four elements - Earth, Air, Fire, and Water - into your space. For example, you could represent Water with a chalice, Air with a feather, Fire with a candle, and Earth with a bowl of salt or a potted plant.

Creating an Atmosphere

Consider how to make your space more conducive to meditation and ritual work. Soft lighting, perhaps from candles or fairy lights, can create a calming atmosphere. You might want to use incense or essential oils to bring in soothing fragrances. Comfortable seating, like a cushion or a mat, will help you maintain focus during longer periods of meditation or ritual work.

Music or nature sounds can also be a powerful way to create a sacred atmosphere. Soft, instrumental music, or the sounds of waves, wind, or forest noises can help you disconnect from the outside world and focus on your inner journey.

Maintaining Your Space

It's not enough to simply set up your sacred space; you must also maintain it. Regularly clean your space, both physically and energetically. Recharge your crystals, replace your candles when they burn out, and freshen up your fragrances as needed. Keeping your sacred space clean and vibrant will reinforce your connection to it and make your practices more effective.

Creating a sacred space is a deeply personal and transformative process. It is an act of devotion to your spiritual path and a commitment to your growth as a white witch. As you spend time in this sacred space, you will find that it becomes imbued with your energy and intentions, becoming a powerful catalyst for your journey towards embodying purity, healing, and light.

Chapter 14: The Seasons and White Witchcraft

Our natural world functions in cycles. Day transitions into night, and the moon phases wax and wane. Similarly, the seasons rotate in an endless dance of transformation, each carrying its unique energy and influence. For the white witch, the changing seasons are not just changes in the weather or shifts in daylight, they are spiritual transitions that affect our energy, our rituals, and our connections to purity, healing, and light.

The Spiritual Significance of Seasons

In many cultures, the year is viewed as a Wheel, with the seasons marking critical points along its cycle. The cycle of the seasons is symbolic of life's cycle – birth, growth, death, and rebirth. For white witches, these cycles are potent times for working with the energies of purity, healing, and light.

Winter, with its long nights and cold temperatures, is a season of introspection and contemplation. It's a time to retreat inward, to meditate and reflect. As the world around us falls into a deep slumber, we can connect more deeply with our inner selves. It's a time of purity, a time to clear away the old and make way for the new.

Spring is the season of rebirth and renewal. It's a time when the world awakens from its winter slumber, bursting forth with life and potential. It's a time of healing, of growth, and a time to bring new plans and projects into the light.

Summer, with its long days and warm temperatures, is a season of fullness and abundance. It's a time to rejoice in the power of the sun, to celebrate life and growth. It's a time to connect with the light, the energy of the universe, and to channel this energy into our own lives.

Autumn, with its cooler temperatures and changing colors, is a season of harvest and completion. It's a time to reap the rewards of our efforts, to give thanks for the abundance in our lives. It's a time of transition, a time to prepare for the introspection of winter.

Winter: The Season of Purity

Winter is a season of introspection and contemplation. As the world outside grows cold and dark, we are encouraged to turn inward, to retreat into the warmth and light within us. This is a powerful time to perform purity rituals. Winter's energy encourages us to shed our old selves and prepare for the rebirth that comes with spring. It's a time to purify our thoughts, our emotions, and our spirit.

One powerful winter ritual for embodying purity involves a cleansing snow bath. After a fresh snowfall, stand outside (appropriately dressed for the weather, of course), and scoop a handful of clean snow. As you hold it, visualize any negative energies, any impurities in your life, being drawn into the snow. When you're ready, throw the snow away from you, physically and symbolically casting off these impurities.

Spring: The Season of Healing

Spring is a time of renewal, growth, and rebirth. As the world around us springs to life, so too can our spirits. Spring's energy is invigorating, pulsating with life and potential. This makes it a potent time for healing rituals.

One powerful spring ritual for healing involves connecting with the energy of new life. Find a quiet spot in nature where you can observe the new growth - whether it's a budding tree, a flowering plant, or a patch of green grass. Sit comfortably and meditate on this new life, feeling its vibrant energy. Visualize this energy as a healing light, absorbing it into yourself, allowing it to permeate every cell of your body, healing and revitalizing you.

Summer: The Season of Light

Summer is a season of abundance, growth, and light. With its long days and warm temperatures, summer is a time to celebrate the light both outside us and within us. This makes it a potent time for rituals connecting with light.

One powerful summer ritual for embracing the light involves sun gazing. Find a quiet spot outdoors during sunrise or sunset. As you watch the sun, feel its radiant energy, its light, and warmth. Visualize this light entering your body, filling you with its radiant energy. Remember, the light you see outside you is also within you.

Autumn: The Season of Transition

Autumn is a season of transition and completion. As the world prepares for winter's rest, we too can take this time to complete projects, to reap the rewards of our efforts, and to give thanks for the abundance in our lives. Autumn's energy encourages us to reflect on our journey, to honor our achievements, and to let go of what no longer serves us.

One powerful autumn ritual involves creating a gratitude altar. Collect items that symbolize the blessings in your life and arrange them on a small table or shelf. Each item should represent something you're grateful for. Spend a few moments each day at your altar, giving thanks for these blessings.

The cycle of the seasons provides a powerful framework for the practice of white witchcraft. By understanding the spiritual energy of each season, we can align our rituals and meditations to these natural rhythms, enhancing our connection to purity, healing, and light. As we move through the Wheel of the Year, let us honor each season's unique energy, celebrating the continuous cycle of birth, growth, death, and rebirth. For it is in this cycle that we find the true magic of life.

Chapter 15: Connecting with Nature

For the white witch, nature is not merely a source of raw materials for spells or a backdrop for rituals. It is a sacred space, a living entity that is interconnected with all forms of life, including ourselves. Its rhythms are our rhythms; its health, our health. Therefore, connecting with nature is a vital aspect of our journey towards embodying purity, healing, and light.

The first step in connecting with nature is understanding its profound significance. Consider how our ancestors lived: they were intimately tied to the cycles of nature. The turning of the seasons dictated when they planted and harvested crops, the movements of the stars were their calendar and clock, the patterns of animal behavior offered insights into the state of their environment. Their very survival depended on this deep understanding and connection with the natural world.

In our modern world, it's all too easy to forget our intrinsic link to nature. We live in temperature-controlled homes, buy food from grocery stores, and spend a large portion of our time engrossed in digital screens. Yet beneath all our advancements and conveniences, the connection remains. Like an echo from our ancestors, it reminds us that we are not separate from the earth and its other inhabitants.

The Elemental Connection

At the heart of white witchcraft lies an understanding of the four classical elements: Earth, Air, Fire, and Water. Each element symbolizes different aspects of nature and ourselves. By connecting with these elements, we tap into their power, wisdom, and energy.

Earth represents stability, fertility, and physical nourishment. It is the ground beneath our feet and the food that sustains us. To connect with the Earth, spend time in natural settings like forests, gardens, or parks. Touch the soil, hug a tree, plant seeds, or walk barefoot on grass. Feel the energy of the Earth, steady and nurturing, flowing into you.

Air stands for intellect, communication, and movement. It's the breath that gives us life and the winds that cleanse our environment. Connect with the Air by observing the wind, listening to its whispers, or practicing mindful breathing. Feel the life-giving oxygen filling your lungs, and as you exhale, release any negative thoughts and feelings.

Fire symbolizes transformation, passion, and will. It's the warmth of the sun and the flame that cooks our food. To connect with Fire, you can safely observe a candle flame, a fireplace, or a bonfire. Feel the warmth on your skin and acknowledge the transformative power of Fire, capable of turning wood into ash, darkness into light.

Water embodies emotion, intuition, and healing. It's the rain that quenches the Earth's thirst and the rivers that carry life. Connect with Water by observing its forms—rivers, lakes, rain, or even a filled bathtub. You can meditate by a water body or cleanse your physical self in a ritual bath, acknowledging the healing and purifying powers of Water.

Forest Bathing: Shinrin-yoku

A practice that can assist you in reconnecting with nature is Shinrin-yoku, or "forest bathing." This Japanese concept involves immersing yourself in a forest environment and using all five senses to experience nature. Studies have shown that forest bathing can reduce stress levels, improve mood, boost the immune system, and lower blood pressure.

Choose a local forest or wooded area to visit. As you enter, leave behind your distractions and worries. Breathe deeply, taking in the scent of the leaves and earth. Listen to the wind rustling the leaves, the songs of the birds, and the quiet that only nature can provide. Reach out and touch the rough bark of a tree, or the softness of a leaf. If it's safe, taste a wild berry or the freshness of a stream. Let nature soak into your soul.

Connecting Through Rituals and Spells

Rituals and spells can also serve as powerful tools to connect with nature. You can conduct rituals to honor the change of seasons, using materials that symbolize each time of the year. For example, a spring ritual might involve seeds and flowers to symbolize new beginnings, while a fall ritual could involve leaves or harvested produce to symbolize abundance and gratitude.

Nature-based spells, such as those involving herbs, crystals, or moon phases, are another way to connect with nature's power. When conducting these spells, it's crucial to do so with respect and not take more from nature than necessary. Always remember that the intent behind your actions matters significantly in white witchcraft.

Reconnecting with nature isn't just a one-time event—it's a continual process of engagement, respect, and gratitude.

As we deepen our connection with the natural world, we not only draw closer to our ancestral roots, but we also enhance our practices as white witches.

In doing so, we learn to embody the purity found in a dewdrop on a leaf, the healing echoed in the continuous cycle of the seasons, and the light mirrored in the dawn of a new day. Thus, through nature, we find ourselves and our place in this intricately woven web of life.

Chapter 16: The Journey Ahead

As we bring this exploration of white witchcraft to a close, it's essential to remember that your journey, your path, is yours alone to tread. Witchcraft, in its many variations, is a deeply personal practice, but the realm of white witchcraft, with its focus on purity, healing, and light, presents a unique perspective on the world and the energies around us. Now, with newfound knowledge and understanding, you are better equipped to navigate your path in the Craft, embracing the principles that resonate with your authentic self.

Your journey into white witchcraft has only just begun. Like the path of a river that winds its way through the landscape, your path will not be straight and unwavering. There will be bends, there will be rapids, and there will be times of serene tranquility. Each phase of the journey, each bend in the river, brings its own lessons and challenges. Embrace them with an open mind and a willing spirit.

Always remember, as you walk this path, you are not alone. You are part of an unbroken line of witches, healers, seers, and wise ones who have tread this path before you. You walk in their footsteps, guided by their wisdom and the wisdom of the divine universal energy that binds all living things.

One of the most important lessons that we hope you take away from this book is that of continuous growth and learning. The Craft is not a destination; it is a journey. With every step you take, every ritual you perform, every meditation you delve into, you are growing, changing, and deepening your understanding of yourself and the world around you. Embrace this process of growth and change, for it is a vital part of your path as a white witch.

Being a white witch is about embodying purity, promoting healing, and shining light into the world. As you step into your role as a healer, remember that healing is not only about mending wounds but also about creating spaces for growth, renewal, and transformation.

You will be a beacon of light, driving away shadows and illuminating the path for others. This role comes with a significant responsibility, and it's essential to be mindful of your intentions and actions. Your impact on others and the world around you is profound. Make sure it is positive, uplifting, and nurturing.

Additionally, never underestimate the importance of grounding yourself in the world around you. Nature is our greatest teacher. It can show us the cycles of life and death, growth and decay, and the eternal balance between light and dark. Spend time in nature whenever possible. Observe the subtle shifts in the seasons, the quiet wisdom of the trees, the gentle whisper of the wind. All of these can offer you insights and wisdom that cannot be found elsewhere.

Do not forget the sacred spaces you have created during your journey. These spaces, filled with your energy and intentions, are the wellsprings of your power. Treat them with reverence and respect, and they will serve you well in your practices.

Remember, too, the tools and symbols you have learned about. They are not just objects; they are extensions of your will and channels for your energy. Choose them wisely and handle them with care. They are your allies and partners in your work.

As you continue your journey, you may encounter challenges. You may face doubts, distractions, or even hostility. However, remember the lessons of the white witch: purity, healing, and light. These principles will guide you through the darkest times and lead you back into the light. Trust in them, trust in yourself, and trust in the wisdom of the universe.

Being a white witch is not a static state; it is a dynamic, evolving process. As you continue to grow, learn, and experience, your understanding of the Craft will deepen, your skills will grow, and your connection to the divine will strengthen. Never stop learning, never stop questioning, and never stop growing.

As you walk this path, remember: you are a white witch. You embody purity, you bring healing, and you radiate light. You are part of the universe, and the universe is part of you. Carry this knowledge in your heart as you continue your journey, and let it guide you on your path.

This is not the end; this is the beginning. The rest of your journey lies ahead, waiting for you to explore and discover. We wish you the best on this beautiful journey, and may you always find the light, even in the darkest of nights. Bright blessings to you, now and always.

Dandelion Lemonade

Pick 1/4 of dandelion and wash them and rinse them well and dra well.

Put them in a jug.

Juice 3 lemons and add them to the dandilions with sweetener of your choice (honey) about 4 TBSP.

Then add 2 quarts of water. Give it a stir. Put a lid on it and in the fridge for at least 3.4 Hours overnight is ideal.

dandelions have Vit A.C K E.B. dandelions are good for the skin and provide relief for aches and pains.

Printed in Great Britain
by Amazon

2 quarts = 1.893 Litres